THE INNER COACH

Rewire the source code of your inner voice

BRETT ODGERS

Published by

Business Growth Advisors

SYDNEY, AUSTRALIA

MDA Publishing
Higginbotham Rd
Gladesville, NSW, 2111
Australia

Book Layout © 2021

The inner coach -- 1st ed.
ISBN 978-0-6450942-2-0

Find Brett Odgers on Facebook
business@brettodgers.com.au

The material in this journal is for general use only and not intended to provide specific advice for particular circumstances. It should not be relied on as the basis for any significant decision, specifically with regards to your physical or mental wellbeing. If issues arise from the journaling process, please seek professional help. Readers should seek professional advice, where appropriate before taking any action or making a significant decision arising from your work in this book.

THE CULTURE
COACH

"Whether you think
you can, or you
can't... You are
right"

– Henry Ford

The power of the inner Coach

Dan Jansen was a once in a generation athlete.... He was the most naturally gifted speed skater the USA team had ever seen The only problem.... He'd never won an Olympic gold medal.

In fact, he was developing a reputation as one of the biggest chokers in the sports history. And it wasn't entirely his fault. He had chosen the 500m speed skating event to specialise in and there was no room for error in this race, in this sport... I mean none. The slightest hiccup and your race was done.

In this sport all eyes were on the Olympic medals, which only come around every 4 years. In this sport you had the perfect storm of pressure. One race, every four years to get everything right. To skate the perfect race and win a medal.

As well as physical conditioning the inner game taking place inside the mind of the competitor had a disproportionately large influence here. The slightest misstep either in the mind or on the ice would send you home without any reward for 4 years of blood, sweat, tears and heartache.

Into this story arrives sports psychologist Dr Jim Loehr, who received a call from dans agent to come work with dan after a disastrous Olympics.

"He will be an Olympic champion if we can get him to fully release his talent and skill. He's had a really terrible situation happen to him and he's struggling. He may go down as the greatest choker in sports history unless we can get him elevated to another plateau with the challenges that he faces."

In his second Olympics at Calgary, he was slated to win an Olympic gold medal in the 500-meter.

On the morning of his race for the gold he received unexpected and devastating news. His sister, jane, who he was very close to, died that morning of leukemia. Nobody knew about it or expected it. Total shock sunk into the tight knit family. You can only imagine the thoughts going through Dans head. He would have walked away from it all to spend a few final moments with his little sister had he have known.

Grief is a total body experience. Your mind, body and soul aches in a way that you didn't think was possible. Unexpected loss is a magnification of epic proportions over expected loss. And it was in this cyclone of emotions and chaos that Dan decided to compete in the final race. Jane would have wanted him to give it

everything he had. And if he managed to win, what a brilliant memorial to his believed sister.

The 500 was not to be that race. He slipped in the first turn.

Four days later he managed to mobile himself to skate in the 1000m, which he did as training for him primary race, the 500.

The mental toughness to do this was immeasurable, but to find himself out in front with a significant margin between him and 2nd was a miracle.

Until a small error occurred. Dan slipped, fell and crashed out, along with his dreams of an Olympic gold medal.

And so, begins the real story of Dan Jansen.

The press were merciless in pestering him. Will you fall again? And with that playing on his mind small mistakes were creeping into his race. And small slips mean big losses in this sport. In one race he was down to 26th, and when Jim started working with him, he just wasn't able to compete at all.

They began work, not just on his physical development, but even more importantly, on his mindset. They kept training logs every day for 2 years, not just race times, diets and gym workouts, they monitored everything. Energy level, sleep quality, emotional even spiritual factors. Everything makes a difference. And especially the stories that are being played out in your head during training. Developing mental toughness and resilience takes the courage to look in places you haven't looked before.

They monitored 21 different factors every day for 2 years coming up to the next Olympic games. And as he began to see patterns, they began to correct them.

One day Jim asked Dan what his inner coach had to say. Dan grimaced. I'm not sure I'd like to tell you that. He's pretty harsh. To be honest he makes the old school Russian gymnastics coaches look like teddy bears. Athletes can be their own harshest critics. And for most people to aspire to leadership the story is the same. Our inner critic is a very harsh taskmaster.

Jim pressed. How would you feel about projecting those voices up onto the jumbotron as you compete?

Dan blushed a little. I wouldn't want anyone to hear that. It's actually a bit embarrassing the things I say in my own head.

And then the penny dropped. That's effectively what's happening as I'm racing.

The loudest voice is telling me I'm stupid, telling me I'll fall again, telling me I'm not good enough to win gold. And he's relentless, cruel and not helping me at all. The only thing he really does is to keep track of all that I haven't done perfectly.

And that's not helping me win gold.

It's time we put a better coach in your head, Jim pushed.

What would be something you'd really like to achieve at the next Olympics. Which would be his final. A medal was all Dan could think about. It was the only thing he hadn't won in his career spanning 4 Olympic games.

In order to do that he'd have to do something that was thought to be impossible. He'd have to do break the 36sec barrier for the 500m. Something that was thought to be physically impossible at the time.

But no one has ever done that? Dan objected. We are going to change your mindset around that. And from that day forward Dan wrote 35:59 on the top on every page of his training journal.

But Jim wanted dan to have a backup. I want you to really compete in the 1000. In fact, I'd like you to write "I love the 1000" on each page as well. But I don't love the 1000 objected Dan. But one day you are going to come up to me and say, Jim I do love the 1000… But it wasn't that day.

Dan went on to break that record three times prior to the Olympics, recording a mind boggling 35:76. A physical limit previously thought impossible was smashed more than once. Dan went into Lillehammer the favourite for the gold.

He even came up to Jim prior and said. "You know what, I really am starting to love the 1000."

Fast forward to the Lillehammer Olympics and Dan has a minor slip in his 500m - primary race. The old Russian gymnastic coach started to get very loud inside his head, nearly as loud as the press who were beginning to write headlines about the greatest choker of all time.

He'd broken all the records for that race but didn't come home with a medal.

But they had 4 days to reset the mind and take the last chance they had to win a medal.

Dan decided to go into that race to express the joy that skating gave him. He wanted to say thank you to everyone that had supported him, and to farewell a sport that he felt had given him so much.

He went into that race with seven other competitors that had faster times than he did.... But he came away with the gold, and the world record.... The relief, the gratitude and the emotion of the win was overwhelming.

An entire nation celebrated with him and today sports greats such as Tony Hawke rate this as the most inspiring sporting performance of all time.

It just goes to show how amazing it is when you start realizing just how much the influence we have over the categories of our thinking and how we feel emotionally. All we have to do is tap in. Make the right inputs and make them regularly. The brain is so plastic, so flexible, so pliable, it will come around. Just like Dan Jansen did.

Your Inner Coach

No matter how inspiring, or how powerful coaching can be for you and your business, there is always one voice that is louder than all the rest.... That voice commands more attention than any other factor.... That's... The voice in your head.

I call that voice your inner coach.

Where does it come from?
It's made up of past experiences, information from childhood, feedback from bosses, colleagues, and friends. And it's not always helpful.

For most of us we know exactly what Dan Jansen is getting at when he said he wouldn't want anyone to hear what his inner voice tells him during a race.

My own inner voice is a total dickhead.... Reminding me when I've not done things perfectly, comparing me to unrealistic standards, ignoring all the good stuff I do... If my inner voice was a person, I would not like him very much, let alone take advice from him.

Yet that's what I do every day. My actions are powerfully shaped by the messages my inner voice is giving me. And that I'm accepting

Lately I've been pondering a question. If I could install the best coach in the world right inside your head, what would he or she say instead? How would the best coach in the world talk to you as you go through your day, build your business, deal with team and customers. What would the best coach in the world say about recovery and rest? And how

different would that be to your current inner coach?

What could we achieve in your business if we rewrote the source code of that coach?

Wouldn't it be cool if you were getting the best coaching advice in the world no matter where you are or how long it is between coaching sessions?

That's an intergenerational influence I'd like to see happen.

So how could I do that?

Here's my theory.

If I could rewrite the source code of that voice in your head and make progress toward it being one of the best coaches in the world. That would impact you for the rest of your life.

You would be walking around with a brilliant, kind, resourceful and positively challenging coach with you everywhere you go. And no one could take that away from you. No circumstance could knock you down.

I really like that idea. Not just for the long term.... But for right now.

Then I started to wonder what this year would be like if you take all the insights, strategies and tactics that we work on together, and your inner coach doesn't resist.

Instead that voice knows the right thing to say at the right time. When to be cautious, when to lean in and when you need to be kind to yourself.

I wonder what kind of results that might create?

I have a suspicion it could be something quite magnificent.

What's your Dan Jansen number? Dan wanted to beat the 36sec mark, so his number was 35.99. He wrote it on every page of his training logs. And what does it mean?

I once worked with a professional Rugby team who decided they wanted to build a completely new culture in their team within 1 year. So their number was 360 and 144. They wanted to be the most legendary team in the clubs 144 history within 360 days. This was written in chalk everywhere. From the boardroom to the gym. Players and admin staff had to walk over these numbers at the front door the building every day as they arrived... And every evening as they returned home... It worked.

What's your I love the 1000 statement? This is the mindset you need to change. It's a bit like an I am statement. What's the statement about what you need to become and the thing you need to learn to love in the pursuit of that?

It turns out, that the fastest way to access the executive functions of the brain is by journaling...

But if you kept a diary you probably knew that already

There is something really amazing about keeping notes and diary entries about your life. Scientists are now discovering that the power of journaling goes far beyond the childhood hobby of so many teenagers.

It's the fastest way to rewire the brain and to make long lasting changes to your behaviour. No wonder so many sports coaches have been asking athletes to track their daily habits. Now we've discovered that tracking the whole person, emotional, physical and even spiritual has huge benefits across other areas of life. Like business.

CEO's and executives are discovering the power and challenge of tracking what's really happening.

For many it becomes one of the most difficult challenges in their personal and professional journey. Discovering automatic behaviours that are holding them back or managing the stories we tell ourselves has become a cornerstone of entrepreneurs and leaders across the world.

The Inner coach journal brings together the power of journaling and coaching in one place. With this 6-week journal you'll not only learn to tame the inner voice, but you'll be challenged with transformational questions, and given space to develop practical actions.

The frameworks in this journal are designed for both discovery and simple actionable exercises that will begin to create a more resourceful inner coach. After all, that voice in your head, your inner coach, is the most powerful force for both change and a lack of it in your life.

It's not important that you do it perfectly, or even every day. It's vital that you simply stay in motion.

Map your daily energy. It could just be that energy management is more effective than time management.

The "Did I Do my Best" wheel helps you track eight important factors in quality of life and work. Score each element. Join the dots and create a visual map of what's happening and where to focus on tomorrow.

Give your day a score in real time. Was it a +2 or a -1 kind of day? You get to decide what qualifies for that score. Tracking it in real time will help you understand how to have more +2 days. And to see what the components of a great day, or a difficult day really are.

Wouldn't it be cool if we could rewrite the source code in your head?

This is your 6-week journal

In this upgraded Inner coach workbook, we'll begin to rewrite the stories in your head your inner coach is telling you.

Take a few minutes out each day to track, in real time, what the coach in your head is doing, saying and influencing you about.

This edition has space for daily goals, as well as what progress you made on those goals. And a daily gratitude finder.

Make your daily goals simple and short. But do identify them. Both personal and work related.

On the weekly scores page there is room for notes, please identify why you gave the day a particular score. Just so you remember in real time.

It's not just work. It's life too.

Track your energy

Pay attention to how your energy level is throughout the day. Then track it in the journal.

Don't worry about making conscious adjustments, let the insights come and take action on them when it's right for you.

I'm beginning to wonder when your peak energy levels are throughout the day. Wouldn't it be cool to use that time to get a lot of important stuff done?

And what are those times in the day when your energy is at its lowest? When everything is harder because you're not at your sharpest. Maybe that's when your body is telling you to take a break. Rest and recover, ready for the next race.

Progress not Perfection

There are only 5 days of journals each week. If you manage to complete 60% of the days, you'll see great progress.

At the end of each week there are self-coaching prompts and worksheets to consider. Complete those that grab your attention. Ignore the others.

You will get some great ideas as you work through this.... I've also included Capture cards for you to name your strategy or project and identify how much it's worth to you. You can even estimate the effort and v's reward on these powerful little cards.

Leave gaps in the days, scribble all sorts of notes all over it. Use coloured pens and get messy. This is your journal, no one else needs to see it... It's just for you. And you don't need to do it in any specific order.

Use it, abuse it... because it's a tool that's never intended to look pristine and pretty. Organised and perfect.... You know by now perfection is a myth.

If you need permission to get messy... really messy. You've got it. Do it backwards if you like. Use all of it or no one of it. Go ahead and lets mess with everything you were taught at school and do it your way.

For some cosmic reason, this works best when you hand write it. Keystrokes on a computer don't seem to cut it when it comes to neuroplasticity. So get the pens, pencils and crayons out and lets go.

You may have noticed. There are only 6 week's worth of journaling in this book... Pssst, lean in close... (whispered voice) I've got plenty more copies where this came from. Lets mess them up too.

Did I do my best to...

Using the Marshall Goldsmith daily questions as a foundation, the "Did I do my best" wheel is a tool to track your overall day.

Step 1. Mark on each indicator line how well you did that day. The centre of the circle representing zero, the outer edge being 10/10

Step 2. Link up the dots using a line to create your own version of the circle. Some days that shape won't look even close to a circle. Other days it might be close but at 30 or 50%.

Step 3. Determine your balance and what to focus on tomorrow.

This is a measure of the balance between important factors in your life and your work.

What's your Rally Cry?

What's the thing that you'd really like to accomplish this year? Not just in your business, but in your life. Is it an income or growth goal, a family dream holiday or a personal achievement?

What's that for you? Let's begin to explore that. And how can we express it simply?

What's your 35:99? (see following Dan Jansen story)

Now... What is the mindset that you need to re-write to make that happen? What's your "I love the 1000"?

It may not come to you straight away, that's o.k. We'll start making the inputs anyway. We'll begin to explore the right inputs to help you install the greatest coach in the world right into your head.

The fast start guide to your daily journal

Do these Sections at the end of the day

Do these Sections at the end of the day

Do these Sections at the beginning of the day

The, In a word exercise

What word first comes to mind about your sleep, diet, mood etc. Don't try to be clever here, simply describe in a word or two each of these important areas. As you start to see patterns you will find that you naturally make small changes in each of these areas. The secret sauce is to continually assess each of these

Today's score

Score your day. Was it a +2 kind of day or a -1 kind of day? You get to make up your own scale here. Trust your first instinct with this score. Here we are looking for patterns. What are the elements that make up a great day, and how many of those do you have in the 6 weeks of this journal? At the end of each week's journal is a page to keep your weekly score and make a few notes on why the day got that score.

If this is taking more than 5 minutes per day, you are overthinking it.... or really enjoying the experience.

Start off with today's goals.

Make them simple and able to be done within the day. Don't be tempted to write your big fat hairy goals in here, they are big picture stuff. Instead list down the things that you want to get done today, activities that will move things forward.

In the morning list do the Another reason to be happy today exercise

Then identify a few things you are grateful for. Again, list out small things. A great conversation, the warmth of your bed, a great cup of coffee, client you enjoy working with.

We now know that identifying what you are grateful for has a direct impact on your happiness hormones. It really does change your brain chemistry. And helps you focus on what's working in your life.

Inner voice, Best coach in the world, the Did I do my best circle and the In a Word exercise should be done at the end of the day.

Inner voice. Notice what messages you are currently paying attention to during the day. They tend to be a bit hard on you and overtly critical. On the right-hand side list out what a great coach would say to you about these thoughts. A coach with perspective, wisdom and insight would give you totally different advice. Now write that down.

Use the slider below that section to estimate how much of your inner voice chat is positive or negative.

The three pillars of resilient leaders

Time management is a constant challenge. But we are beginning to wonder if the real secret might be energy management. The pandemic has shown that working remotely can be even more productive than being in an office, and flexible working hours are a major contributor to that.

Rather than chaining yourself to a desk and forcing yourself to be productive, what if we could work within our natural energy cycles.

We know that different people are at their peak productivity at different times in the day. What if we worked withing those cycles? Things become much easier, results come more quickly, and friction is lower all around.

Awareness

Most people are simply responding to daily situations. By developing your awareness, through the power of journaling, we understand where to put our attention and how to make it most effective. We call that Responding rather than reacting.

Mental toughness

Mental toughness isn't about being hard and strong. The traditional model of toughness isn't as effective as it was once thought to be. It's actually about developing mindful techniques, maintaining your power in any situation and ultimate fuelling a great life.

Without it, it's very easy to drop below the line and indulging in blaming others, making excuses and unnecessary and unhelpful emotion.

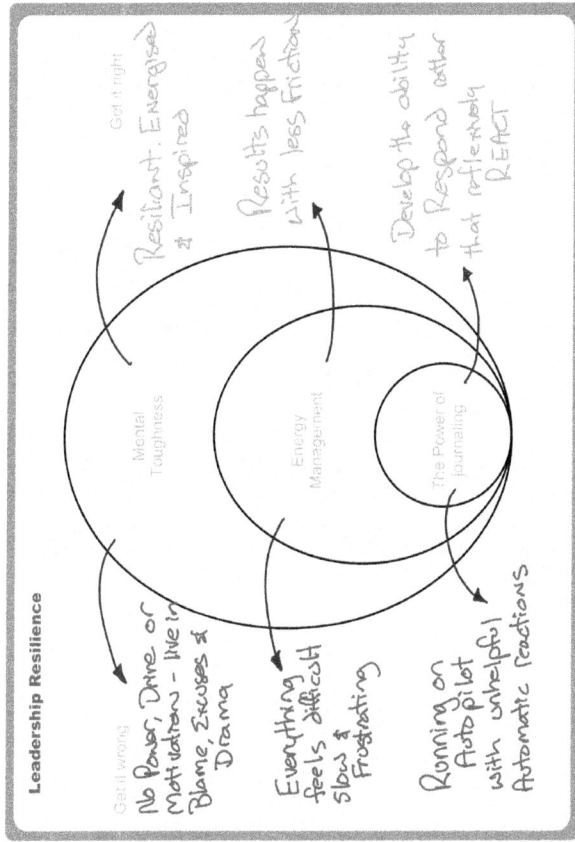

Leadership Resilience

Get it wrong
No Power, Drive or Motivation - live in Blame, Excuses & Drama

Everything feels difficult slow & Frustrating

Running on Auto Pilot with unhelpful Automatic reactions

Mental Toughness

Energy Management

The Power of journaling

Get it right
Resilient, Energised & Inspired

Results happen with less friction

Develop the ability to Respond rather that reflexively REACT

The three rings of resilient leaders are the basis for this journal.

The Legacy Model

What's the big bright future?

I envision a world where people discover that they are more powerful than they can imagine. That they are more abundant, generous, clever, compassionate and entrepreneurial than they thought was possible.

With insight, and guidance and surrounded by the right culture that everyone can leave an imprint on the world that lasts for generations I call than an intergenerational legacy...

My vision is that every one of you become a leader who creates that intergenerational legacy. That means what you do, what you stand for and what you work toward has impact long after you stop working on it. That your legacy will have an impact on the generations that follow. At work, at home and in your community.

My vision:
To create a tsunami of leaders who share & spread inspiring ideas...
Who build successful entrepreneurial businesses & communities where people can be at their best, feel safe, experience trust, work in their genius zone and return home energised and fulfilled.

My mission: To build an organisation that creates transformational change and an environment that supports you with the insight, inspiration and guidance to build whatever you can dream, whatever you can imagine.

I see a world where each of you are empowered to work in your unique, creative strengths.... Where you create cultures that encourage the very best in the people that surround you, and where an abundance of time, money, meaning and connection are generated.

I call than, an intergenerational legacy...

Intergenerational love
Intergenerational wealth
Intergenerational health... &
Intergenerational education

To do that we need to look after three pillars of leadership. This book is all about self-leadership. It's the foundation of many other aspects of success.

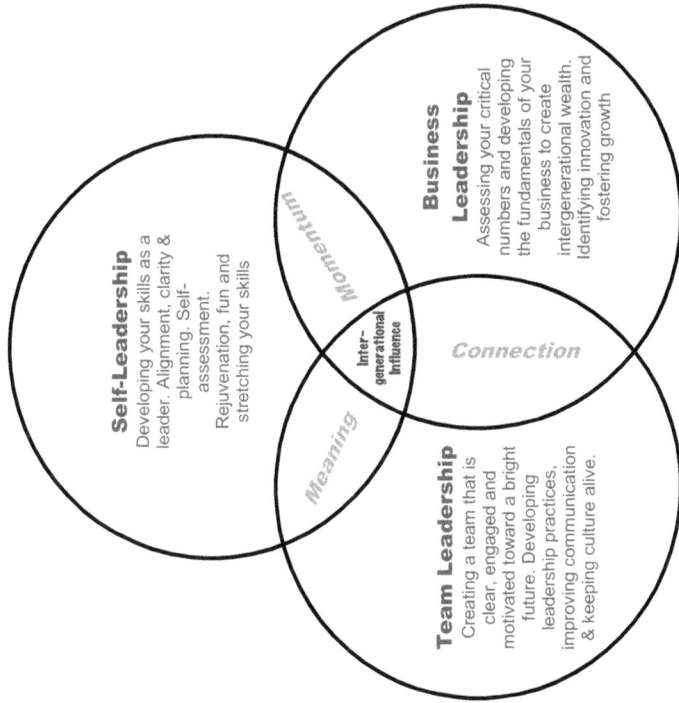

Self-Leadership
Developing your skills as a leader. Alignment, clarity & planning. Self-assessment. Rejuvenation, fun and stretching your skills

Business Leadership
Assessing your critical numbers and developing the fundamentals of your business to create intergenerational wealth. Identifying innovation and fostering growth

Team Leadership
Creating a team that is clear, engaged and motivated toward a bright future. Developing leadership practices, improving communication & keeping culture alive.

Momentum

Meaning

Connection

Inter-generational Influence

Progress not Perfection

An imperfect plan passionately and creatively executed today, is better than a perfect plan next month – *Brett Odgers*

Daily Journal

Today's Score — -2 — -1 — 0 — $+1$ — $+2$

Date:

Did I do my best to...

Set clear goals

Focus on what's working

Make progress toward goals

Seek happiness

Be engaged

Be kind to myself

Find meaning in my day

Build positive relationships

Today's Goals...

Today my Inner voice has been vocal about....
(List some of the messages you've noticed have been on your mind today)

The best coach in the world would say...
(What would the best coaching advice in the world have to say?)

In a word...

My sleep was _____

My diet was _____

My state of mind was _____

Negative ——————— **Positive**

Russian Gym Coach   *World's best Coach*

Another reason to be happy today is... *(what are you grateful for?)* *(What percentage of your inner voice talk has been positive or negative today)*

Energy

High

Low

Morning   Midday / afternoon   Evening

Daily Journal

Today's Score

-2   -1   0   +1   +2

Did I do my best to...

Set clear
goals

Make progress
toward goals

Seek happiness

Focus on what's
working

Be engaged

Be kind
to myself

Find meaning
in my day

Build positive
relationships

Today's Goals...

Today my Inner voice has been vocal about....

(List some of the messages you've noticed have been on your mind today)

The best coach in the world would say...

(What would the best coaching advice in the world have to say?)

Negative ——————— **Positive**

*Russian Gym
Coach*

(What percentage of your inner voice talk has been positive or negative today)

*World's best
Coach*

Another reason to be happy today is... (what are you grateful for?)

In a word...

My sleep was _____

My diet was _____

My state of mind was _____

Energy

High

Low

Morning | Midday / afternoon | Evening

Daily Journal

Today's Score   -2   -1   0   +1   +2

Date:

Did I do my best to...

Set clear goals

Focus on what's working

Make progress toward goals

Seek happiness

Be engaged

Find meaning in my day

Be kind to myself

Build positive relationships

In a word...

My sleep was _____

My diet was _____

My state of mind was _____

Today's Goals...

Today my Inner voice has been vocal about...
(List some of the messages you've noticed have been on your mind today)

The best coach in the world would say....
(What would the best coaching advice in the world have to say?)

Negative ——————————— Positive

Russian Gym Coach   World's best Coach

(What percentage of your inner voice talk has been positive or negative today)

Another reason to be happy today is... (what are you grateful for?)

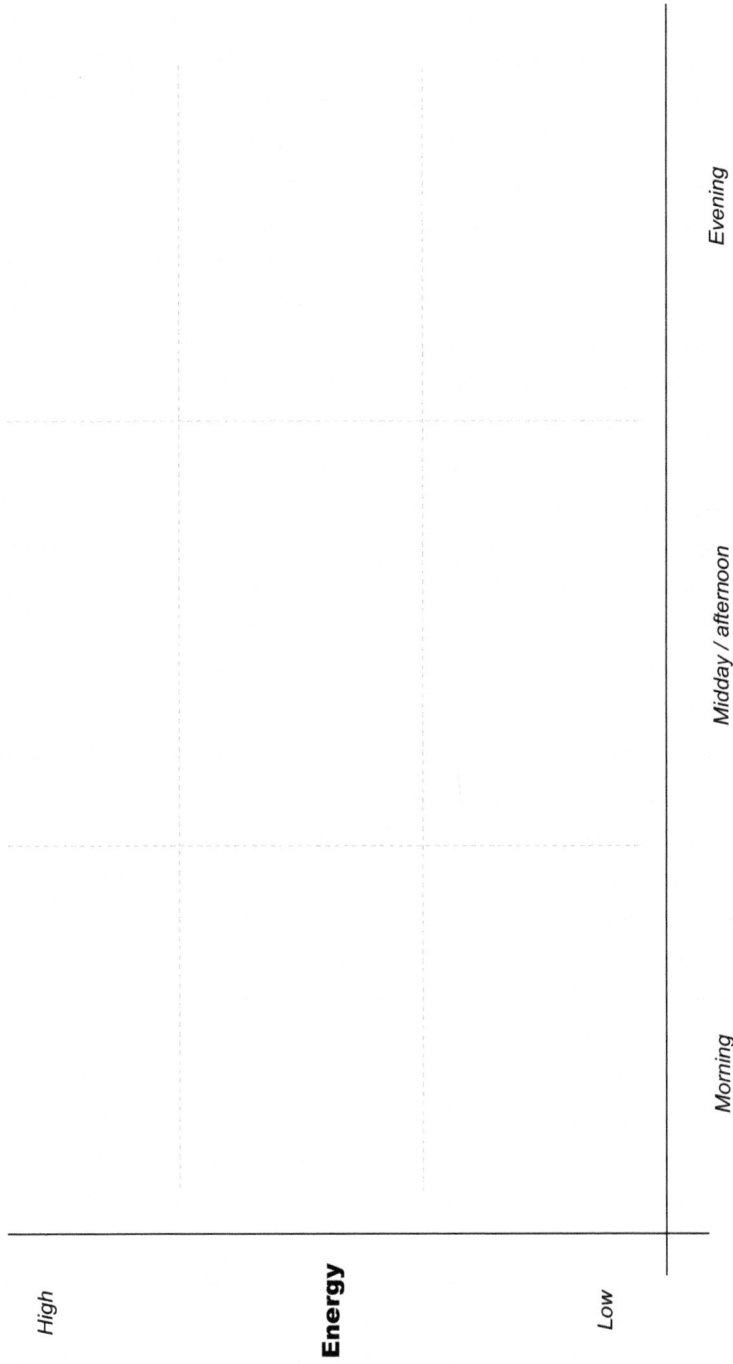

High

Energy

Low

Morning

Midday / afternoon

Evening

Daily Journal

Today's Score

-2   -1   0   +1   +2

Date:

Did I do my best to...

Set clear goals

Make progress toward goals

Focus on what's working

Seek happiness

Be engaged

Be kind to myself

Find meaning in my day

Build positive relationships

In a word...

My sleep was _____

My diet was _____

My state of mind was _____

Today's Goals...

Today my inner voice has been vocal about....
(List some of the messages you've noticed have been on your mind today)

The best coach in the world would say...
(What would the best coaching advice in the world have to say?)

Negative ———————————————— **Positive**

Russian Gym Coach   *(What percentage of your inner voice talk has been positive or negative today)*   *World's best Coach*

Another reason to be happy today is... *(what are you grateful for?)*

High

Energy

Low

Morning   Midday / afternoon   Evening

Daily Journal

Today's Score -2   -1   0   +1   +2

Date:

Did I do my best to...

Set clear goals

Make progress toward goals

Seek happiness

Focus on what's working

Be engaged

Find meaning in my day

Be kind to myself

Build positive relationships

Today's Goals...

Today my Inner voice has been vocal about....
(List some of the messages you've noticed have been on your mind today)

The best coach in the world would say....
(What would the best coaching advice in the world have to say?)

In a word...

My sleep was _____

My diet was _____

My state of mind was _____

Negative ————————————— Positive

Russian Gym Coach   *(What percentage of your inner voice talk has been positive or negative today)*   *World's best Coach*

Another reason to be happy today is... *(what are you grateful for?)*

Energy

High

Low

Morning | Midday / afternoon | Evening

Was it a good day? *(The weekly real time satisfaction index)*   **Week beginning**

	Mon	Tue	Wed	Thurs	Fri	Sat	Sun
+2							
+1							
0							
-1							
-2							
Why this score							

What are your numbers teaching you?

What are your people / family & friends teaching you?

What are your customers & audience teaching you?

I'm Curious...

1. If I did things that felt more like me. What would I do differently?

2. What activities are taking up my time... that I resent? *(follow-up question below...)*

3. Who would LOVE to do the activities I resent doing? *(Another follow-up question below...)*

4. How could I do a great handover of those activities and ensure this person rocks the job?

5. If I decided never to retire, what could I do with my time? *(follow-up question below...)*

6. How could I start doing more of that now?

7. What could I put in place to allow me to go off the grid for a few weeks?

Actions

Capture Cards — Capture your ideas and projects using this simple tool

Strategy Name

Next Steps

Potential Result

Effort Level

Strategy name

Next Steps

Potential Result

Effort Level

Strategy name

Next Steps

Potential Result

Effort Level

Strategy name

Next Steps

Potential Result

Effort Level

How many requests don't I make, that if I did, could change my world?

Did I do my best to…

Set clear
goals

*Focus on what's
working*

*Make progress
toward goals*

Seek happiness

Be engaged

*Find meaning
in my day*

*Be kind
to myself*

*Build positive
relationships*

Today's Goals…

Today my Inner voice has been vocal about….
(List some of the messages you've noticed have been on your mind today)

The best coach in the world would say…
(What would the best coaching advice in the world have to say?)

In a word…

My sleep was _____

My diet was _____

My state of mind was _____

My mood was _____

Negative ————————— Positive

*Russian Gym
Coach*

(What percentage of your inner voice talk has been positive or negative today)

*World's best
Coach*

Another reason to be happy today is … (what are you grateful for?)

Daily Energy Map

Date:

Energy

High

Low

Morning   Midday / afternoon   Evening

Did I do my best to…

-2   -1   0   +1   +2

Set clear goals

Make progress toward goals

Seek happiness

Be engaged

Find meaning in my day

Build positive relationships

Be kind to myself

Focus on what's working

Today's Goals…

Today my Inner voice has been vocal about….
(List some of the messages you've noticed have been on your mind today)

The best coach in the world would say….
(What would the best coaching advice in the world have to say?)

Negative ——————————— *Positive*

Russian Gym Coach

World's best Coach

(What percentage of your inner voice talk has been positive or negative today?)

Another reason to be happy today is… (what are you grateful for?)

In a word…

My sleep was _____

My diet was _____

My state of mind was _____

My mood was _____

Daily Energy Map

Energy

High

Low

Morning   Midday / afternoon   Evening

Did I do my best to...

Set clear goals

Make progress toward goals

Seek happiness

Focus on what's working

Be engaged

Be kind to myself

Find meaning in my day

Build positive relationships

Today's Goals...

Today my Inner voice has been vocal about....
(List some of the messages you've noticed have been on your mind today)

The best coach in the world would say....
(What would the best coaching advice in the world have to say?)

Negative ——————————————— Positive

Russian Gym Coach   *World's best Coach*

(What percentage of your inner voice talk has been positive or negative today)

Another reason to be happy today is... (what are you grateful for?)

In a word...

My sleep was _____

My diet was _____

My state of mind was _____

My mood was _____

Daily Energy Map

Date:

Energy

High

Low

Morning Midday / afternoon Evening

Did I do my best to...

Today's Goals...

Set clear
goals

Make progress
toward goals

Focus on what's
working

Seek happiness

Be engaged

Find meaning
in my day

Be kind
to myself

Build positive
relationships

Today my Inner voice has been vocal about....
(List some of the messages you've noticed have been on your mind today)

The best coach in the world would say....
(What would the best coaching advice in the world have to say?)

In a word...

My sleep was _____

My diet was _____

My state of mind was _____

My mood was _____

Negative ——————————————— Positive

Russian Gym
Coach

World's best
Coach

(What percentage of your inner voice talk has been positive or negative today)

Another reason to be happy today is... *(what are you grateful for?)*

Daily Energy Map

High

Energy

Low

Morning   Midday / afternoon   Evening

Today's score   -2   -1   0   +1   +2

Did I do my best to…

Set clear goals

Focus on what's working

Make progress toward goals

Seek happiness

Be engaged

Find meaning in my day

Build positive relationships

Be kind to myself

Today's Goals…

Today my Inner voice has been vocal about…
(List some of the messages you've noticed have been on your mind today)

The best coach in the world would say…
(What would the best coaching advice in the world have to say?)

Negative ——————————— Positive

Russian Gym Coach   World's best Coach

(What percentage of your inner voice talk has been positive or negative today)

Another reason to be happy today is… (what are you grateful for?)

In a word…

My sleep was _____

My diet was _____

My state of mind was _____

My mood was _____

Daily Energy Map

Date:

Energy

High

Low

Morning   Midday / afternoon   Evening

Mon	Tue	Wed	Thurs	Fri	Sat	Sun

+2

+1

0

-1

-2

Why this score

I'm Curious...

1. What if I did the opposite for 48 hours?

2. What do I spend a silly amount of money on? How might I scratch my own itch?

3. What would I do/have/be if I had $10 million? What's my real Target Monthly Income? (TMI)

4. What's a list of the worst things that could happen? Could I get back to where I am today?

5. If I could only work 2 - 4 hours per week on my business, what would I prioritise?

6. What's the least crowded channel to get my message out?

7. What if I couldn't pitch my product directly? How could I tell a story about a client who has had great results instead?

Actions

are they currently getting. And on the RHS box what % you'd like them to get. The boxes below are for the actions you need to take in relation to those.

What's Frustrating?

What's working?

What's Fascinating?

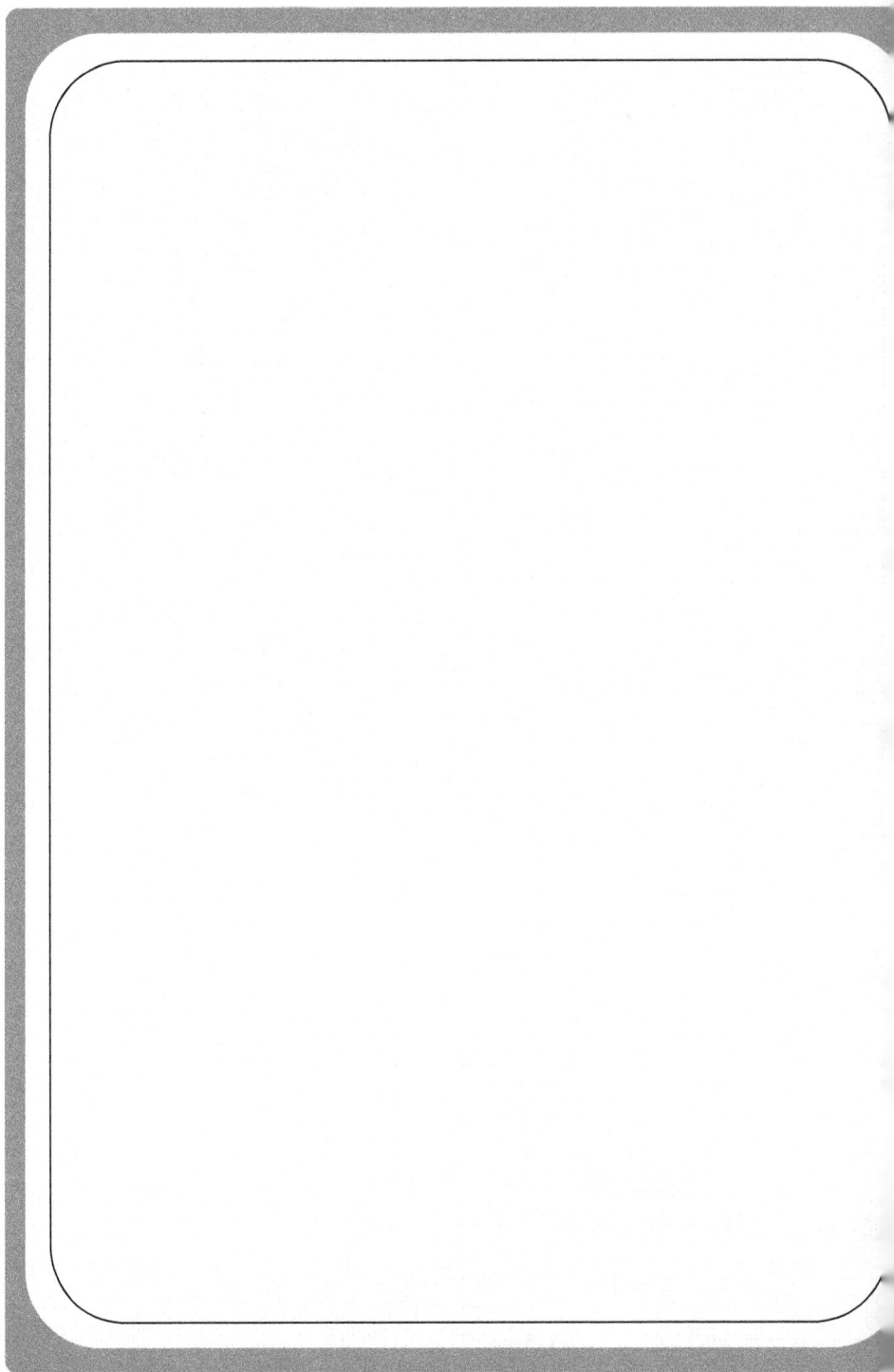

Capture your ideas and projects using this simple tool

Strategy Name

Next Steps

Potential Result

Effort Level

Strategy name

Next Steps

Potential Result

Effort Level

Strategy name

Next Steps

Potential Result

Effort Level

Strategy name

Next Steps

Potential Result

Effort Level

Week 3

The most powerful technology ever invented.... is storytelling

Daily Journal

Today's Score

_____ -2 _____ -1 _____ 0 _____ +1 _____ +2

Date:

Did I do my best to...

Set clear goals

Make progress toward goals

Focus on what's working

Seek happiness

Be engaged

Be kind to myself

Find meaning in my day

Build positive relationships

In a word...

My sleep was _____

My diet was _____

My state of mind was _____

Today's Goals...

Today my Inner voice has been vocal about....
(List some of the messages you've noticed have been on your mind today)

The best coach in the world would say....
(What would the best coaching advice in the world have to say?)

_____

Negative _____ Positive

(What percentage of your inner voice talk has been positive or negative today?)

Russian Gym Coach

World's best Coach

Another reason to be happy today is... (what are you grateful for?)

High

Energy

Low

Morning   Midday / afternoon   Evening

Daily Journal

Today's Score ___-2___ ___-1___ ___0___ ___+1___ ___+2___

Did I do my best to...

Set clear
goals

Make progress
toward goals

Seek happiness

Focus on what's
working

Be engaged

Be kind
to myself

Find meaning
in my day

Build positive
relationships

In a word...

My sleep was _____

My diet was _____

My state of mind was _____

Today's Goals...

Today my inner voice has been vocal about....
(List some of the messages you've noticed have been on your mind today)

The best coach in the world would say....
(What would the best coaching advice in the world have to say?)

Negative ——————————————— **Positive**

Russian Gym
Coach

World's best
Coach

(What percentage of your inner voice talk has been positive or negative today)

Another reason to be happy today is... *(what are you grateful for?)*

Energy

High

Low

Morning   Midday / afternoon   Evening

Daily Journal

Today's Score

-2 —— -1 —— 0 —— +1 —— +2

Date:

Did I do my best to...

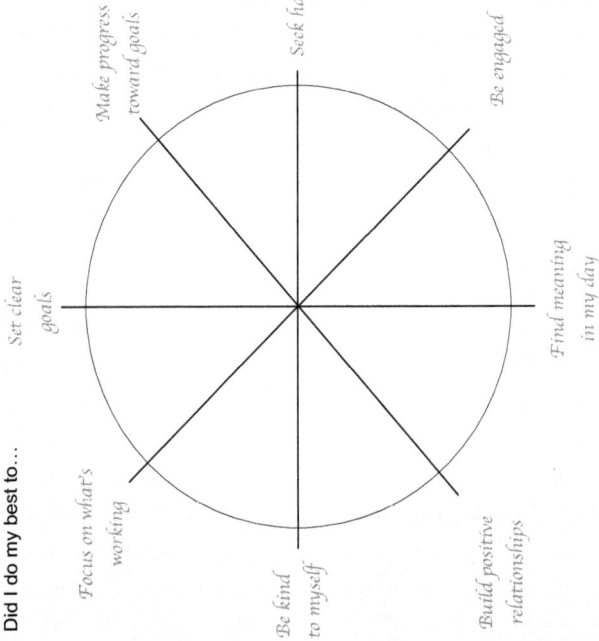

Set clear goals

Focus on what's working

Make progress toward goals

Seek happiness

Be engaged

Find meaning in my day

Be kind to myself

Build positive relationships

Today's Goals...

Today my inner voice has been vocal about....
(List some of the messages you've noticed have been on your mind today)

The best coach in the world would say....
(What would the best coaching advice in the world have to say?)

In a word...

My sleep was _____

My diet was _____

My state of mind was _____

Negative ————————————— Positive

Russian Gym Coach

World's best Coach

(What percentage of your inner voice talk has been positive or negative today)

Another reason to be happy today is . . . (what are you grateful for?)

Energy

High

Low

Morning

Midday / afternoon

Evening

Daily Journal

Did I do my best to...

Set clear goals

Make progress toward goals

Focus on what's working

Seek happiness

Be engaged

Be kind to myself

Find meaning in my day

Build positive relationships

In a word...

My sleep was _____

My diet was _____

My state of mind was _____

Today's Goals...

Today my Inner voice has been vocal about....
(List some of the messages you've noticed have been on your mind today)

The best coach in the world would say....
(What would the best coaching advice in the world have to say?)

Negative ——————————— Positive

(What percentage of your Inner voice talk has been positive or negative today)

Russian Gym Coach   World's best Coach

Another reason to be happy today is.. *(what are you grateful for?)*

Energy

High

Low

Morning   Midday / afternoon   Evening

Daily Journal

Today's Score

−2   −1   0   +1   +2

Date:

Did I do my best to...

Set clear
goals

Focus on what's
working

Make progress
toward goals

Seek happiness

Be engaged

Be kind
to myself

Find meaning
in my day

Build positive
relationships

Today's Goals...

Today my Inner voice has been vocal about....
(List some of the messages you've noticed have been on your mind today)

The best coach in the world would say...
(What would the best coaching advice in the world have to say?)

Negative ——————————— Positive

Russian Gym Coach   *World's best Coach*

(What percentage of your inner voice talk has been positive or negative today)

Another reason to be happy today is ... *(what are you grateful for?)*

In a word...

My sleep was _____

My diet was _____

My state of mind was _____

Energy

High

Low

Morning | Midday / afternoon | Evening

Was it a good day? *(The weekly real time satisfaction index)*

Week beginning

	Mon	Tue	Wed	Thurs	Fri	Sat	Sun
+2							
+1							
0							
-1							
-2							

Why
this
score

	Neglected	Weak	Strong	Superpower
Health				
Wealth				
Relationships				
Meaning in your work				
Happiness & joy				

I'm Curious...

1. **Am I hunting big game, or field mice?** *(Am I spending my energy for a small feed or a big feed? A lion can catch either, it takes the same energy)*

2. **Which of the solutions in front of me would make all the rest easier, or irrelevant?**

3. **What would this look like if it were easy?**

4. **How can I most effectively throw money at this problem..... to improve my quality of life?**

5. **If I acknowledged all the small wins in my life and my work. What would the first 3 wins be?**

6. **What do you already know you need to do to solve this?**

7. **What aren't you seeing in this situation... Yet?**

Actions

Strategy Name

Next Steps

Effort Level

Potential Result

Strategy name

Next Steps

Effort Level

Potential Result

Strategy name

Next Steps

Effort Level

Potential Result

Strategy name

Next Steps

Effort Level

Potential Result

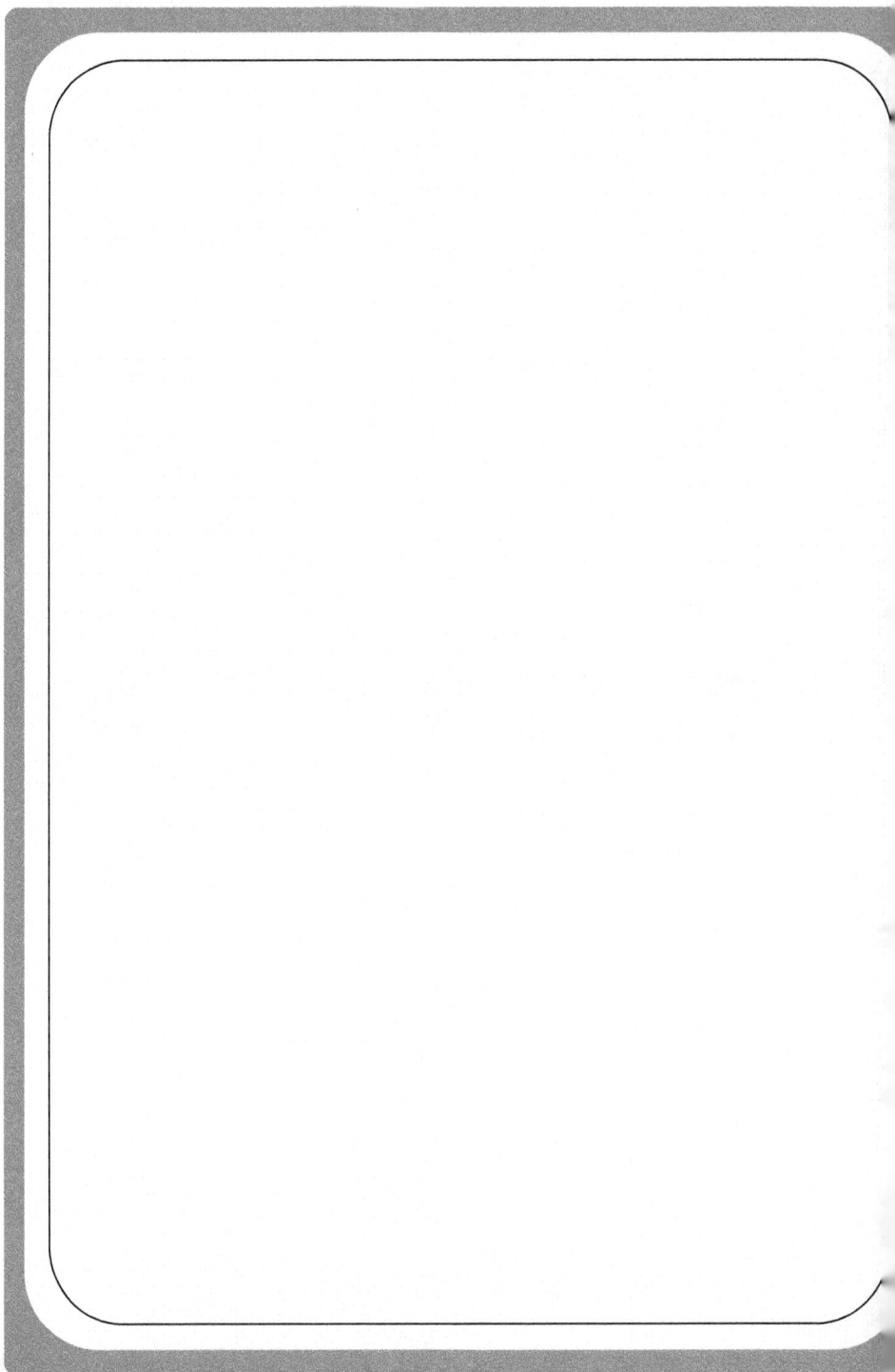

Champions do extra.

It's the little extra things that champions do that makes the difference. Every person on the planet can be a champion to someone – *Brett Odgers*

Date:

Today's Goals...

Set clear goals

Make progress toward goals

Seek happiness

Focus on what's working

Be engaged

Be kind to myself

Find meaning in my day

Build positive relationships

Today my Inner voice has been vocal about....
(List some of the messages you've noticed have been on your mind today)

The best coach in the world would say...
(What would the best coaching advice in the world have to say?)

In a word...

My sleep was _____

My diet was _____

My state of mind was _____

My mood was _____

Negative ——————————— Positive

Russian Gym Coach   *World's best Coach*

(What percentage of your inner voice talk has been positive or negative today)

Another reason to be happy today is ... (what am you grateful for?)

Daily Energy Map

Energy

High

Low

Morning

Midday / afternoon

Evening

Today's Goals...

The best coach in the world would say....
(What would the best coaching advice in the world have to say?)

Make progress
toward goals

Set clear
goals

Seek happiness

Focus on what's
working

Be engaged

Find meaning
in my day

Be kind
to myself

Build positive
relationships

Today my Inner voice has been vocal about....
(List some of the messages you've noticed have been on your mind today)

Negative ──────── *Positive*

*Russian Gym
Coach*

*World's best
Coach*

(What percentage of your inner voice talk has been positive or negative today)

Another reason to be happy today is... *(what are you grateful for?)*

In a word...

My sleep was _____

My diet was _____

My state of mind was _____

My mood was _____

Daily Energy Map

Date:

High

Energy

Low

Morning   Midday / afternoon   Evening

Today's Goals...

Set clear
goals

Make progress
toward goals

Seek happiness

Focus on what's
working

Be engaged

Be kind
to myself

Find meaning
in my day

Build positive
relationships

Today my Inner voice has been vocal about....
(List some of the messages you've noticed have been on your mind today)

The best coach in the world would say...
(What would the best coaching advice in the world have to say?)

Negative —————————————— Positive

(What percentage of your inner voice talk has been positive or negative today)

Russian Gym
Coach

World's best
Coach

Another reason to be happy today is ... (what are you grateful for?)

In a word...

My sleep was _____

My diet was _____

My state of mind was _____

My mood was _____

Daily Energy Map

Date:

High

Energy

Low

Morning   Midday / afternoon   Evening

Date

Today's Goals...

The best coach in the world would say....
(What would the best coaching advice in the world have to say?)

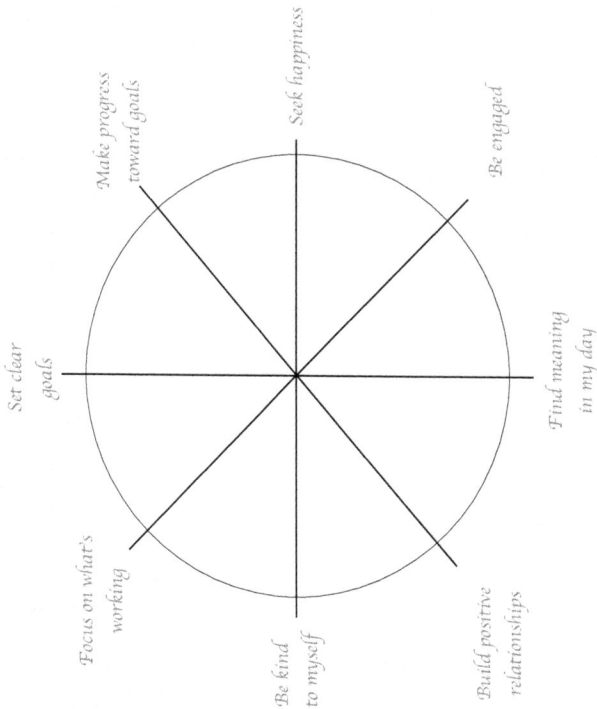

Today my Inner voice has been vocal about....
(List some of the messages you've noticed have been on your mind today)

Make progress toward goals

Seek happiness

Set clear goals

Be engaged

Focus on what's working

Find meaning in my day

Be kind to myself

Build positive relationships

Negative ——————————————— Positive

Russian Gym Coach   *(What percentage of your inner voice talk has been positive or negative today)*   *World's best Coach*

Another reason to be happy today is ... (what are you grateful for?)

In a word...

My sleep was _____

My diet was _____

My state of mind was _____

My mood was _____

Daily Energy Map

Date:

High

Energy

Low

Morning   Midday / afternoon   Evening

−2   −1   0   +1   +2

Today's Goals...

Set clear
goals

Make progress
toward goals

Seek happiness

Focus on what's
working

Be engaged

Be kind
to myself

Find meaning
in my day

Build positive
relationships

The best coach in the world would say...
(What would the best coaching advice in the world have to say?)

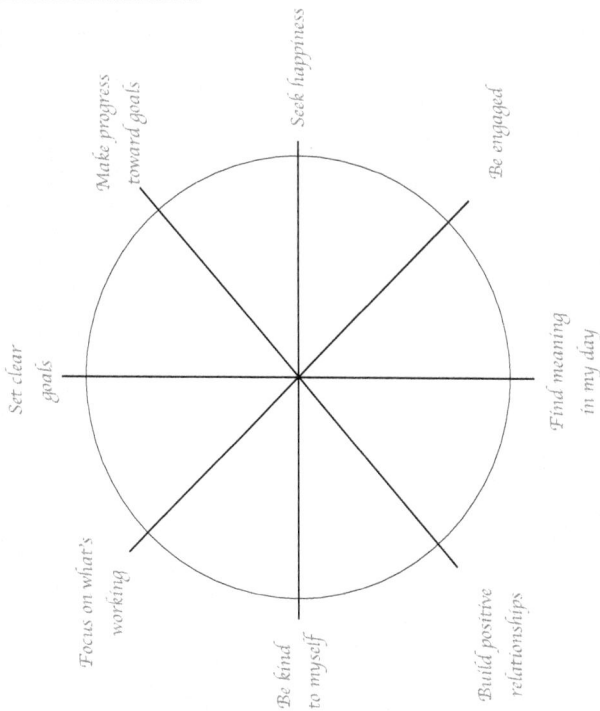

Today my Inner voice has been vocal about....
(List some of the messages you've noticed have been on your mind today)

Negative ——————————————— Positive

Russian Gym
Coach

World's best
Coach

(What percentage of your inner voice talk has been positive or negative today)

Another reason to be happy today is ... *(what are you grateful for?)*

In a word...

My sleep was _____

My diet was _____

My state of mind was _____

My mood was _____

Daily Energy Map

Date:

High

Energy

Low

Morning   Midday / afternoon   Evening

	Mon	Tue	Wed	Thurs	Fri	Sat	Sun
+2							
+1							
0							
-1							
-2							
Why this score							

5 Drivers of your business

Rate each of your drivers. Which one would make the biggest difference if you improved it?

	Neglected	Weakness	Strength	Superpower
New Biz				
Converting opportunities				
Leadership / team / culture				
Low Friction operations				
Growth & Acquisitions				

1	**2**	**3**
Respond rather than React	Manage your internal state	Seek Clarity
4	**5**	**6**
Challenge assumptions	Rejuvenation and recovery time	Practice gratitude & focus on wins

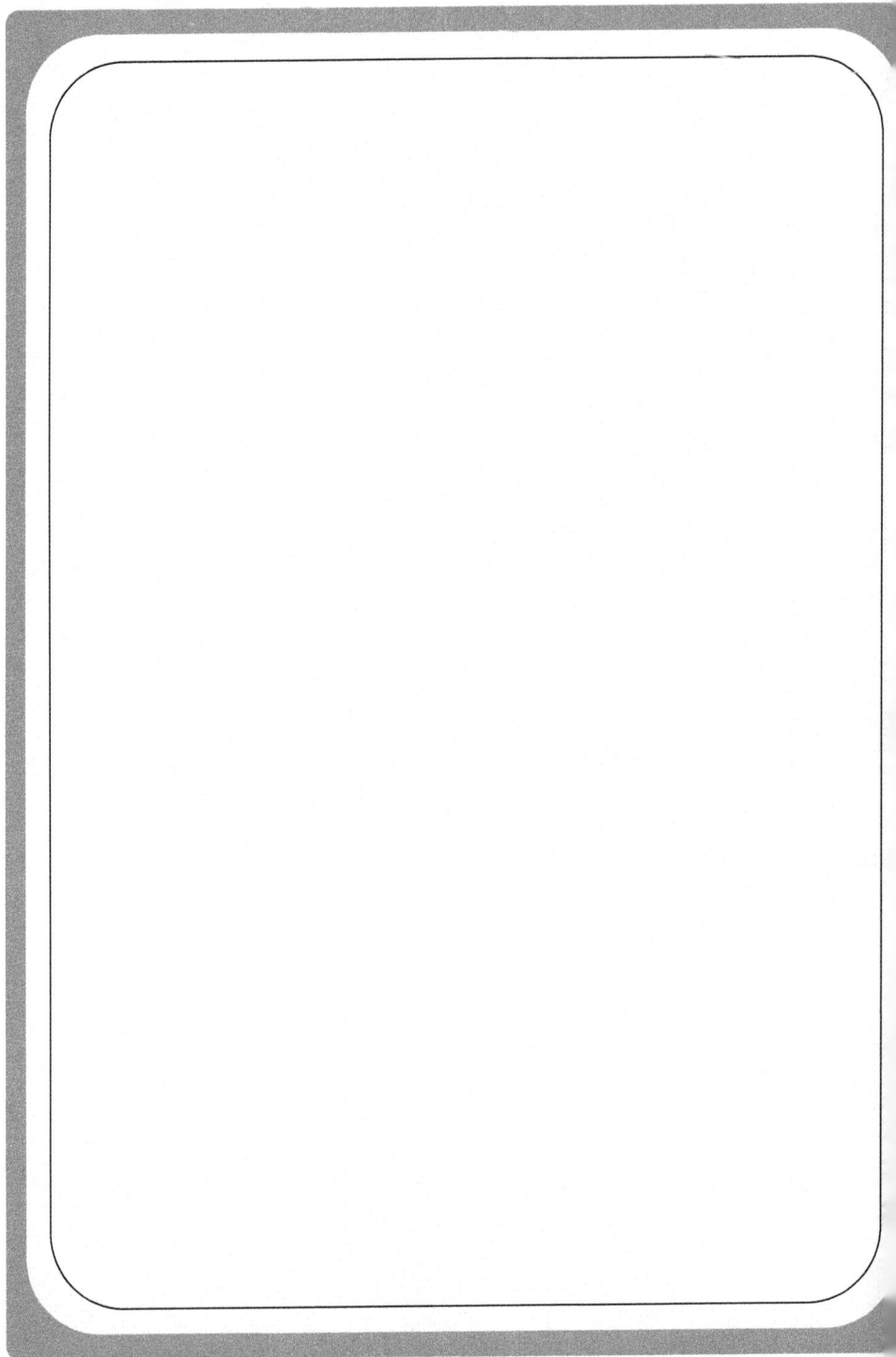

The secret is to stay in motion

A body that is in motion will find itself subject to all kinds of unexpected outcomes, some great, others unwelcome. All human progress relies on motion. The only failure possible is to stop. No motion, no results. That's called Precession, it's an immutable physical law – Brett Odgers

Today's Goals...

Make progress toward goals

Seek happiness

Set clear goals

Be engaged

Focus on what's working

Find meaning in my day

Be kind to myself

Build positive relationships

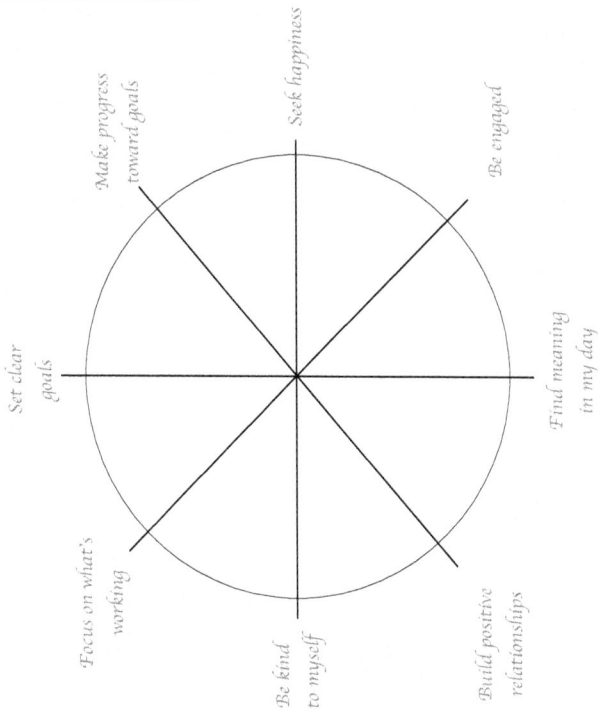

The best coach in the world would say....
(What would the best coaching advice in the world have to say?)

Today my Inner voice has been vocal about....
(List some of the messages you've noticed have been on your mind today)

Negative _____ Positive

(What percentage of your inner voice talk has been positive or negative today)

Russian Gym Coach

World's best Coach

Another reason to be happy today is ... *(what are you grateful for?)*

In a **word**...

My sleep was _____

My diet was _____

My state of mind was _____

My mood was _____

Daily Energy Map

Date:

High

Energy

Low

Morning   Midday / afternoon   Evening

Today's Goals…

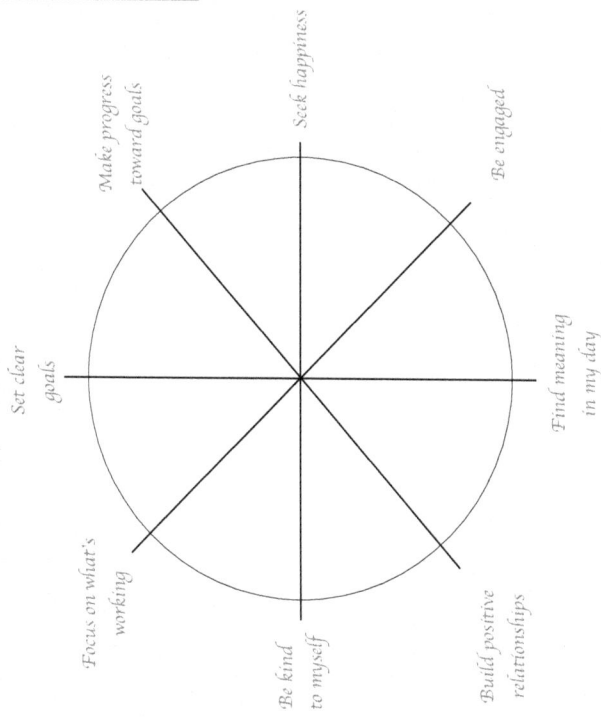

The best coach in the world would say….
(What would the best coaching advice in the world have to say?)

Today my Inner voice has been vocal about….
(List some of the messages you've noticed have been on your mind today)

Make progress toward goals

Set clear goals

Seek happiness

Be engaged

Focus on what's working

Find meaning in my day

Be kind to myself

Build positive relationships

In a word…

My sleep was _____

My diet was _____

My state of mind was _____

My mood was _____

Negative ——————————————— Positive

Russian Gym Coach   World's best Coach

(What percentage of your inner voice talk has been positive or negative today)

Another reason to be happy today is … *(what are you grateful for?)*

Daily Energy Map

Date:

High

Energy

Low

Morning — Midday / afternoon — Evening

Today's Goals...

Set clear
goals

Make progress
toward goals

Seek happiness

Focus on what's
working

Be engaged

Find meaning
in my day

Be kind
to myself

Build positive
relationships

Today my Inner voice has been vocal about....
(List some of the messages you've noticed have been on your mind today)

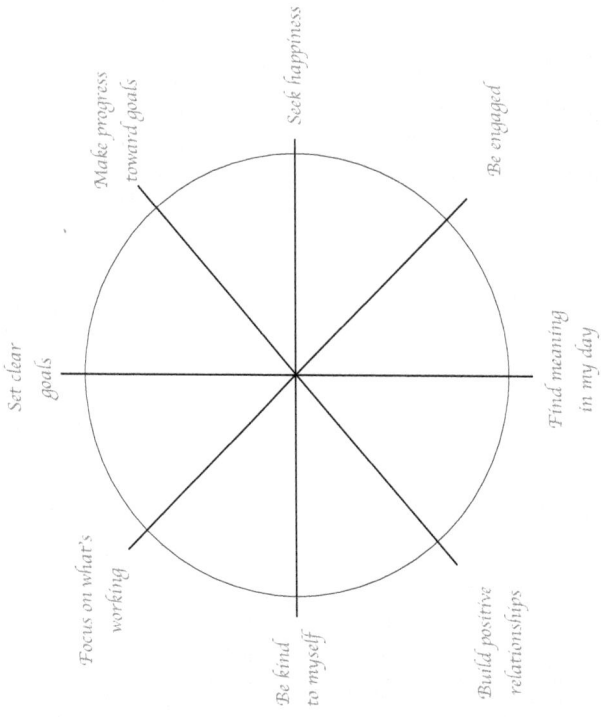

The best coach in the world would say...
(What would the best coaching advice in the world have to say?)

Negative ——————————————— Positive

Russian Gym
Coach

World's best
Coach

Another reason to be happy today is... *(what are you grateful for?)*

In a **word**...

My sleep was _____

My diet was _____

My state of mind was _____

My mood was _____

(What percentage of your inner voice talk has been positive or negative today)

Daily Energy Map

Date:

Energy

High

Low

Morning   Midday / afternoon   Evening

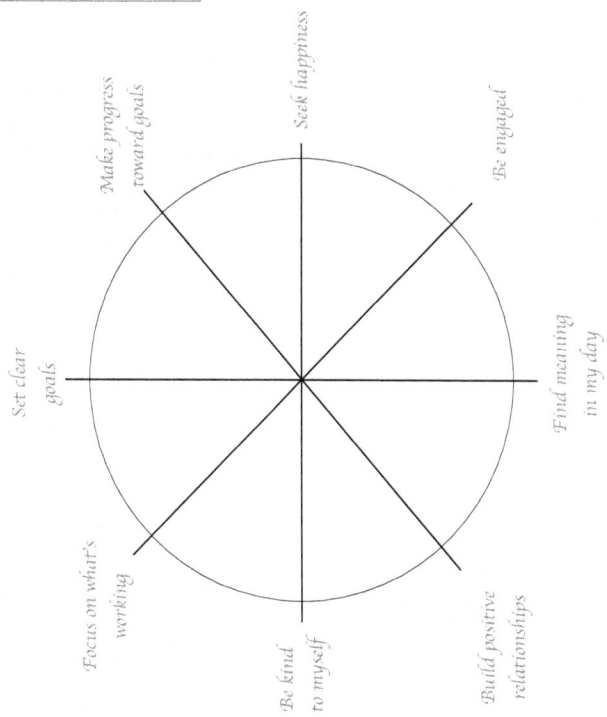

Today's Goals...

The best coach in the world would say....
(What would the best coaching advice in the world have to say?)

Today my Inner voice has been vocal about....
(List some of the messages you've noticed have been on your mind today)

Make progress
toward goals

Set clear
goals

Seek happiness

Be engaged

Focus on what's
working

Find meaning
in my day

Be kind
to myself

Build positive
relationships

In a word...

My sleep was _____

My diet was _____

My state of mind was _____

My mood was _____

Negative ———————————— **Positive**

*Russian Gym
Coach*   *World's best
Coach*

(What percentage of your inner voice talk has been positive or negative today)

Another reason to be happy today is... (what are you grateful for?)

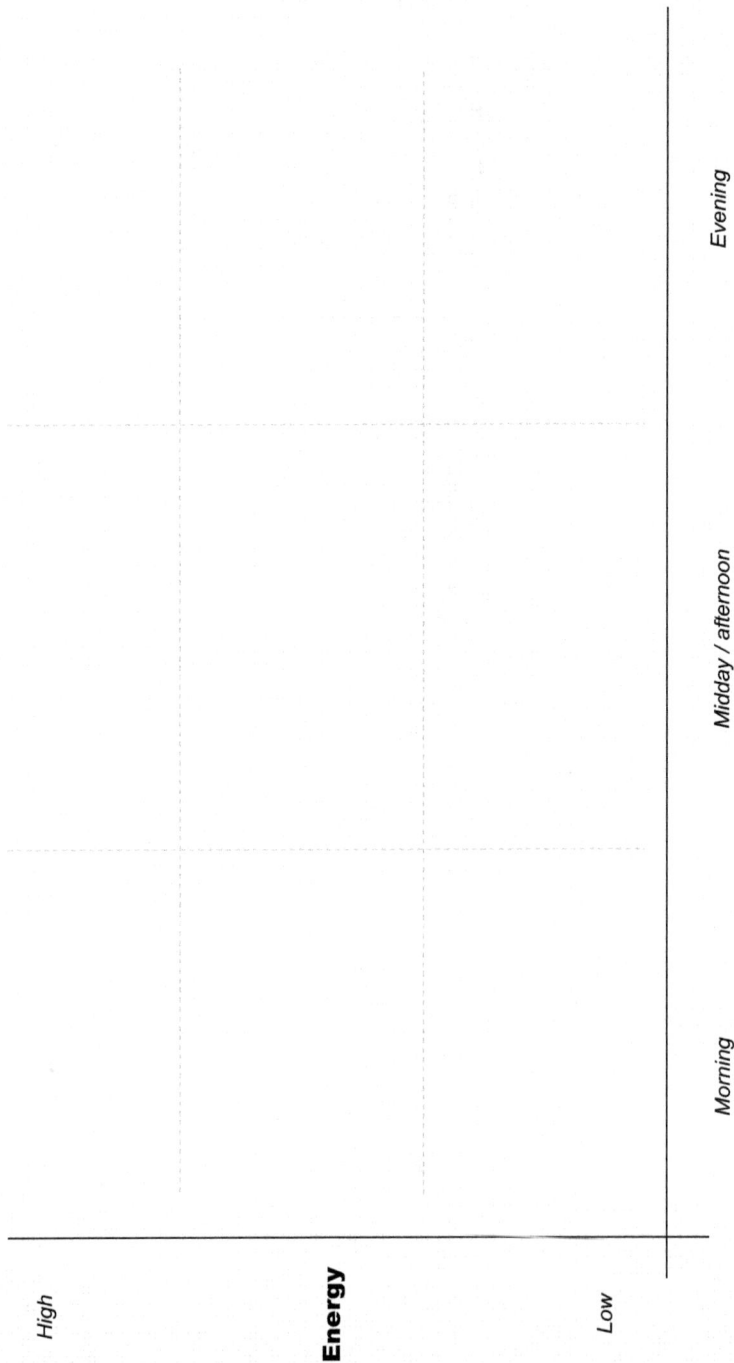

Daily Energy Map

Date:

High

Energy

Low

Morning   Midday / afternoon   Evening

Today's Goals...

Set clear
goals

Make progress
toward goals

Seek happiness

Focus on what's
working

Be engaged

Be kind
to myself

Find meaning
in my day

Build positive
relationships

Today my Inner voice has been vocal about....
(List some of the messages you've noticed have been on your mind today)

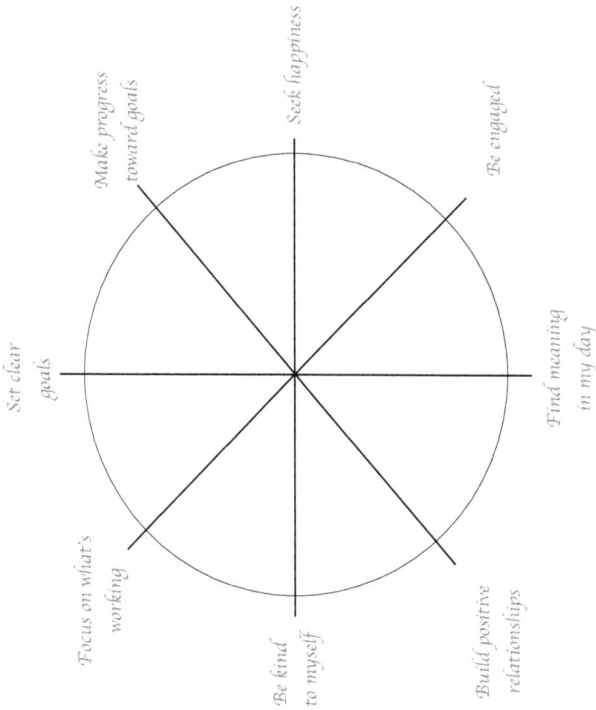

The best coach in the world would say...
(What would the best coaching advice in the world have to say?)

In a word...

My sleep was _____

My diet was _____

My state of mind was _____

My mood was _____

Negative ————————————————— *Positive*

Russian Gym   (What percentage of your inner voice talk has been positive or negative today)   *World's best*
Coach   *Coach*

Another reason to be happy today is... (what are you grateful for?)

Daily Energy Map

Energy

High

Low

Morning   Midday / afternoon   Evening

	Mon	Tue	Wed	Thurs	Fri	Sat	Sun
+2							
+1							
0							
-1							
-2							
Why this score							

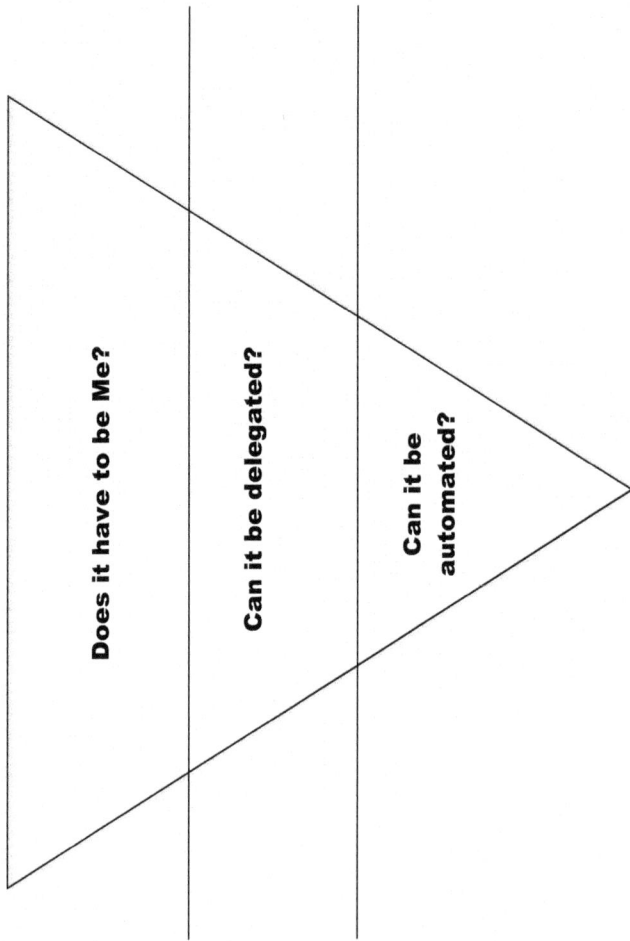

Does it have to be Me?

Can it be delegated?

Can it be automated?

Q. *What isn't being done today, that if it could, would totally transform the business?*

Other questions

Q. *Name one achievement in your business over the past 12 months that has had a significant positive impact on the way your business operates?*

Q. *What unfinished projects do you currently have in your business?*

Q. *Do you have a mission and is it clear to everyone in your business right now?*

Q. *In the next 90 days, what is the most significant thing you wish to achieve in your business?*

Q. *What guidance would you consider to be most valuable?*

Capture Cards – Capture your ideas and projects using this simple tool

Strategy Name

Next Steps

Effort Level

Potential Result

Strategy name

Next Steps

Effort Level

Potential Result

Strategy name

Next Steps

Effort Level

Potential Result

Strategy name

Next Steps

Effort Level

Potential Result

The theory doesn't give a dam if you learn it or not

It will work anyway. Especially if it's one of the immutable laws of the universe. So you may as well pay attention – *Brett Odgers*

Week 6

Today's Goals...

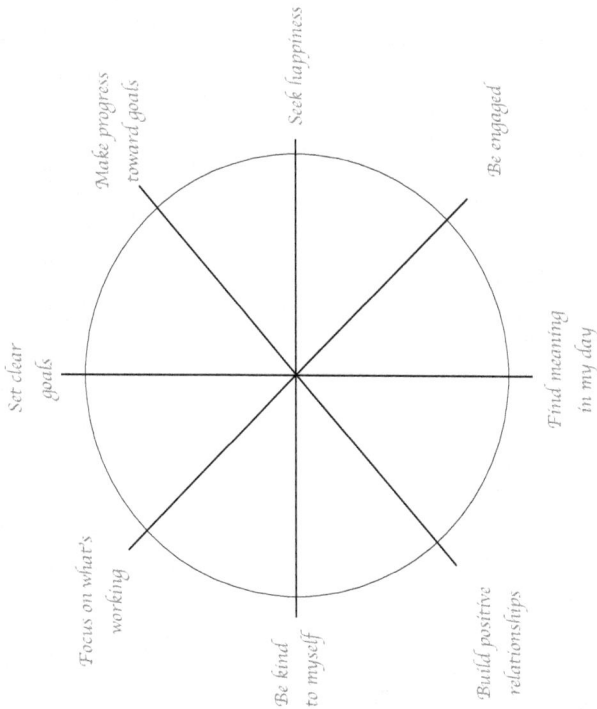

Today my Inner voice has been vocal about....
(List some of the messages you've noticed have been on your mind today)

The best coach in the world would say....
(What would the best coaching advice in the world have to say?)

Set clear goals

Make progress toward goals

Seek happiness

Focus on what's working

Be engaged

Be kind to myself

Find meaning in my day

Build positive relationships

In a word...

My sleep was _____

My diet was _____

My state of mind was _____

My mood was _____

Negative _____ *Positive*

Russian Gym Coach　　　　　　　　　　　　*World's best Coach*

(What percentage of your inner voice talk has been positive or negative today)

Another reason to be happy today is... *(what are you grateful for?)*

Daily Energy Map

Energy

High

Low

Morning

Midday / afternoon

Evening

Today's Goals…

Set clear
goals

Make progress
toward goals

*Focus on what's
working*

Seek happiness

Be engaged

*Be kind
to myself*

*Find meaning
in my day*

*Build positive
relationships*

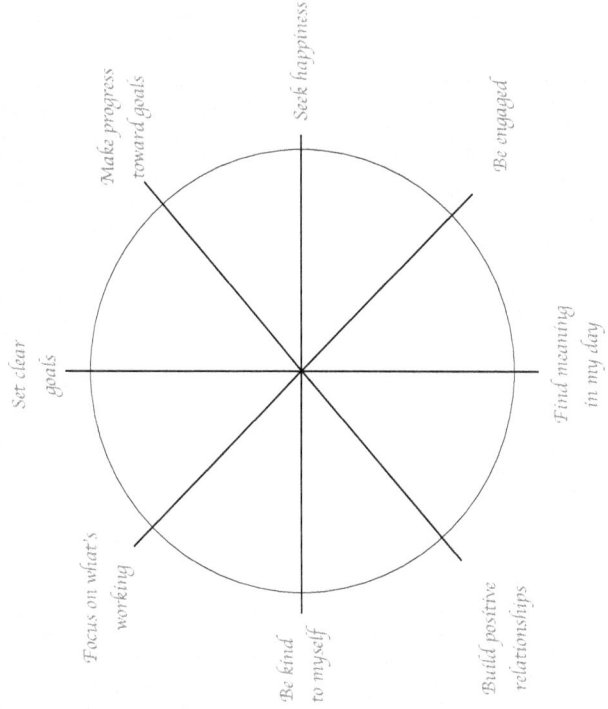

The best coach in the world would say….
(What would the best coaching advice in the world have to say?)

Today my Inner voice has been vocal about….
(List some of the messages you've noticed have been on your mind today)

Negative ——————————— **Positive**

(What percentage of your inner voice talk has been positive or negative today)

Russian Gym
Coach

World's best
Coach

Another reason to be happy today is … (what are you grateful for?)

In a word…

My sleep was _____

My diet was _____

My state of mind was _____

My mood was _____

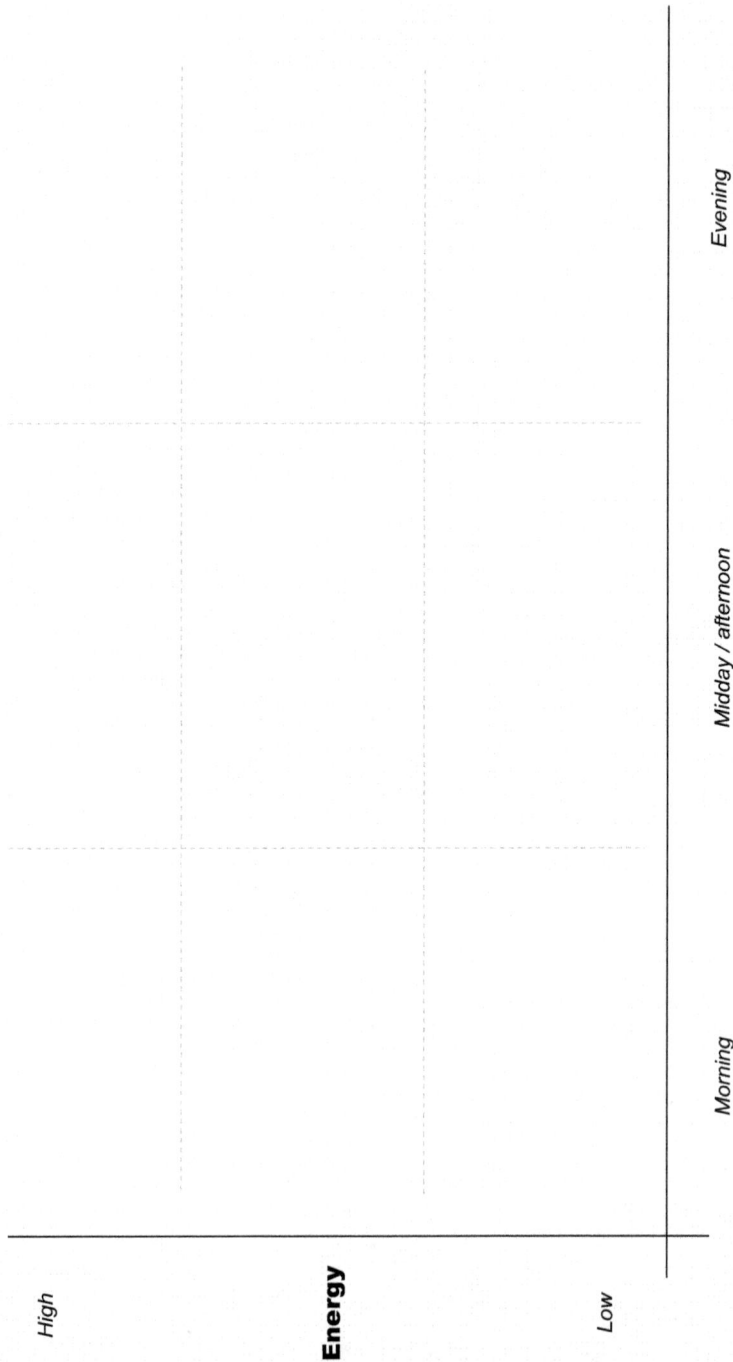

Daily Energy Map

Date:

High

Energy

Low

Morning　　　　　Midday / afternoon　　　　　Evening

Today's Goals...

Set clear
goals

Make progress
toward goals

Seek happiness

Focus on what's
working

Be engaged

Find meaning
in my day

Be kind
to myself

Build positive
relationships

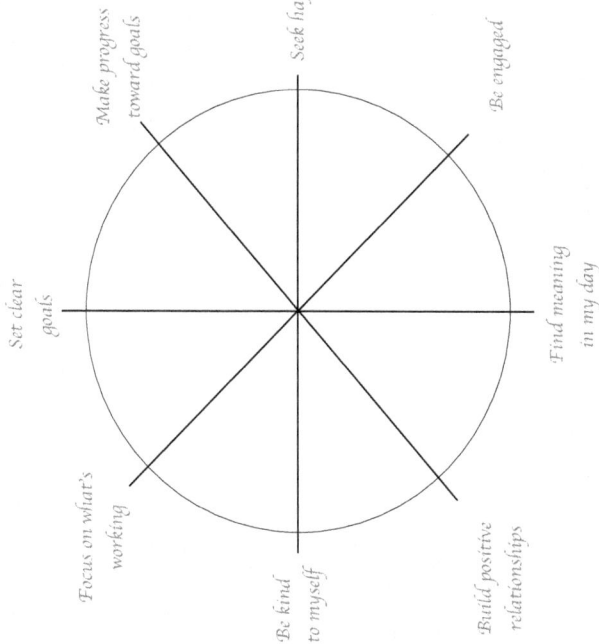

The best coach in the world would say...
(What would the best coaching advice in the world have to say?)

Today my Inner voice has been vocal about....
(List some of the messages you've noticed have been on your mind today)

Negative ———————————— **Positive**

*Russian Gym   World's best
Coach   Coach*

(What percentage of your inner voice talk has been positive or negative today)

Another reason to be happy today is... *(what are you grateful for?)*

In a word...

My sleep was _____

My diet was _____

My state of mind was _____

My mood was _____

Daily Energy Map

High

Energy

Low

Morning   Midday / afternoon   Evening

Today's Goals...

Make progress
toward goals

Seek happiness

Set clear
goals

Be engaged

Focus on what's
working

Find meaning
in my day

Be kind
to myself

Build positive
relationships

The best coach in the world would say....
(What would the best coaching advice in the world have to say?)

Today my Inner voice has been vocal about....
(List some of the messages you've noticed have been on your mind today)

Negative ———————— Positive

Russian Gym Coach   *World's best Coach*

(What percentage of your inner voice talk has been positive or negative today)

Another reason to be happy today is... *(what are you grateful for?)*

In a word...

My sleep was _____

My diet was _____

My state of mind was _____

My mood was _____

Daily Energy Map

Date:

High

Energy

Low

Morning | Midday / afternoon | Evening

-2   -1   0   +1   +2

Today's Goals...

Set clear
goals

Make progress
toward goals

Seek happiness

Focus on what's
working

Be engaged

*Find meaning
in my day*

Be kind
to myself

Build positive
relationships

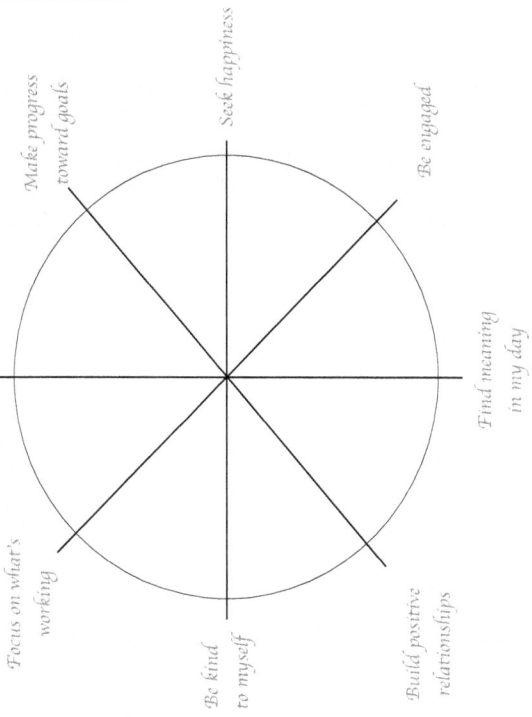

The best coach in the world would say...
(What would the best coaching advice in the world have to say?)

Today my Inner voice has been vocal about....
(List some of the messages you've noticed/have been on your mind today)

In a word...

My sleep was _____

My diet was _____

My state of mind was _____

My mood was _____

Negative ——————————————— Positive

Russian Gym   World's best
Coach   Coach

(What percentage of your inner voice talk has been positive or negative today)

Another reason to be happy today is... (what are you grateful for?)

Daily Energy Map

Date:

High

Energy

Low

Morning   Midday / afternoon   Evening

	Mon	Tue	Wed	Thurs	Fri	Sat	Sun
+2							
+1							
0							
-1							
-2							
Why this score							

Activity Review – What's on your mind right now? Which box does it fit in?

Action Immediately	Reprioritise or Delegate	Hell No!	Someday, Maybe

By this time next year, I would like to have accomplished....

Wouldn't it be cool if this month we could...

Imagine if.... (what would be the coolest, biggest thing you could imagine happening in your life and your business)

What are my Critical Numbers to monitor this month?

The Action Map

Stop doing

Start Doing

Ramp-up

Strategy Name

Next Steps

Effort Level

Potential Result

Strategy name

Next Steps

Effort Level

Potential Result

Strategy name

Next Steps

Effort Level

Potential Result

Strategy name

Next Steps

Effort Level

Potential Result

Light bulb moments

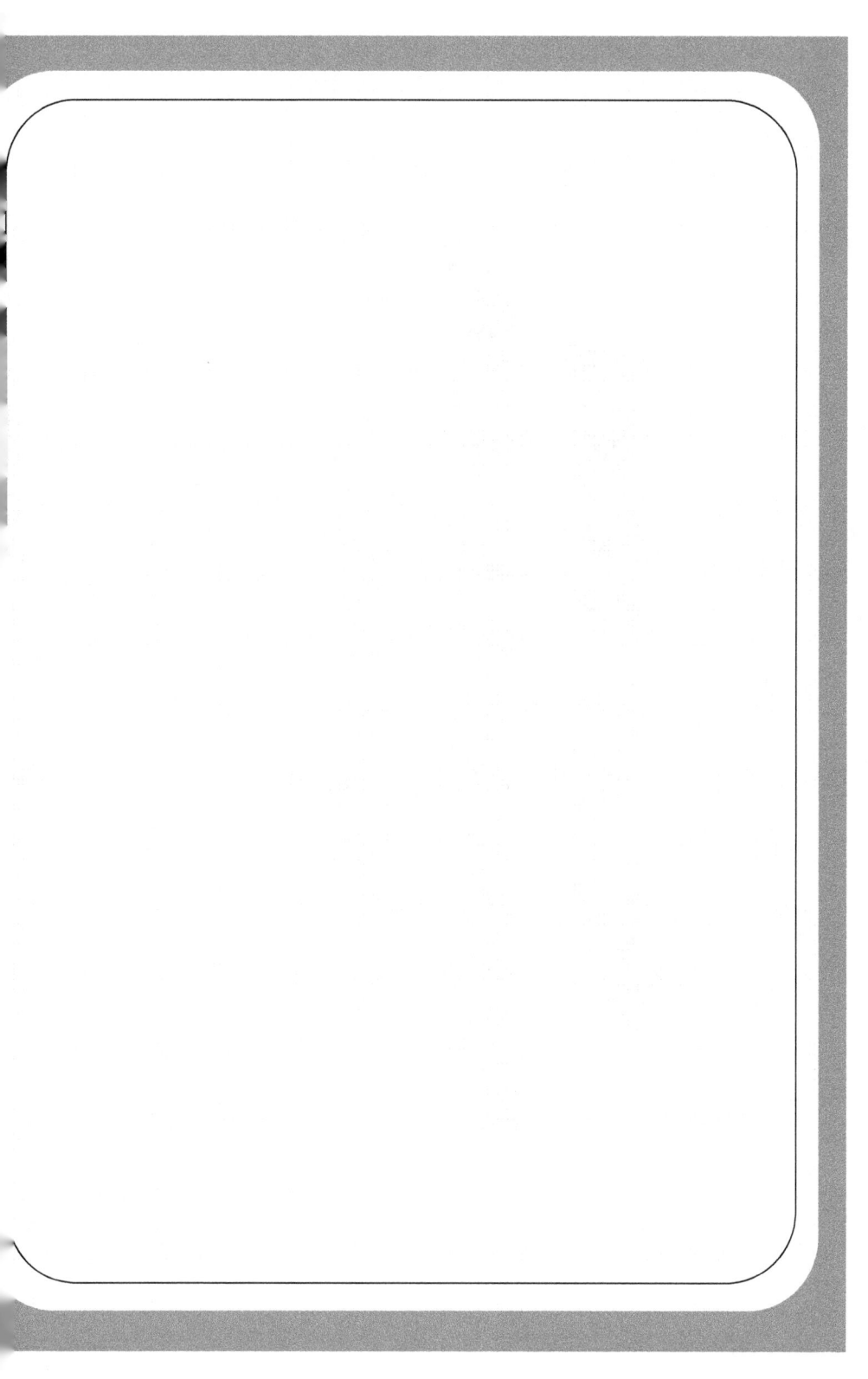

You are a good person who is doing their best.

Never forget this fact. It's not about getting it right all the time. It's simply about giving it your best shot with the time, energy, knowledge and resources you have at hand – *Brett Odgers*